_ □ X

CODING
WITH
DINOSAURS

BY KYLIE BURNS

BELLWETHER MEDIA • MINNEAPOLIS, MN

Imagination comes alive in Express! Transform the everyday into the fresh and new, discover ways to stir up flavor and excitement, and experiment with new ideas and materials. Express! makerspace books: where your next creative adventure begins!

This edition first published in 2024 by Bellwether Media, Inc.

No part of this publication may be reproduced in whole or in part without written permission of the publisher. For information regarding permission, write to Bellwether Media, Inc., Attention: Permissions Department, 6012 Blue Circle Drive, Minnetonka, MN 55343.

Library of Congress Cataloging-in-Publication Data

Names: Burns, Kylie, author.
Title: Coding with dinosaurs / by Kylie Burns.
Description: Minneapolis, MN : Bellwether Media, Inc., 2024. | Series: Express! Adventures in unplugged coding |
  Includes bibliographical references and index. | Audience: Ages 7-13 | Audience: Grades 4-6 | Summary:
  "Information accompanies instructions for various dinosaur-themed activities that demonstrate skills needed for coding.
  The text level and subject matter are intended for students in grades 3 through 8"-- Provided by publisher.
Identifiers: LCCN 2023021277 (print) | LCCN 2023021278 (ebook) | ISBN 9798886875126 (library binding) |
  ISBN 9798886875621 (paperback) | ISBN 9798886877007 (ebook)
Subjects: LCSH: Computer programming--Juvenile literature. | Dinosaurs--Juvenile literature.
Classification: LCC QA76.6115 .B87 2024 (print) | LCC QA76.6115 (ebook) | DDC 005.1--dc23/eng/20230601
LC record available at https://lccn.loc.gov/2023021277
LC ebook record available at https://lccn.loc.gov/2023021278

Text copyright © 2024 by Bellwether Media, Inc. EXPRESS and associated logos are trademarks and/or registered trademarks of Bellwether Media, Inc.

Editors: Sarah Eason and Christina Leaf
Illustrator: Eric Smith
Series Design: Brittany McIntosh
Graphic Designer: Paul Myerscough

Printed in the United States of America, North Mankato, MN.

TABLE OF CONTENTS _ □ X

Coding is **communicating** with computers so they can perform tasks. If you are given an instruction, the first thing that your brain does is receive the message. Because the instruction is in a language you understand, you can follow the steps to perform the task. Coding is a way to communicate **commands** to a computer in its own language through a set of instructions called **code**.

Programmers, or coders, use coding to make programs that tell computers what to do. Programs are sets of codes that create actions.

Like coding with a computer, unplugged coding activities use **sequences**, problem-solving, and **logic**. However, you do not need a computer to do them! The unplugged activities in this book can help you develop skills that will make you an awesome coder. We will use dinosaurs as our theme to make coding even more fun!

LET'S GET STARTED!

SEQUENCE A STEGOSAURUS _ □ X

In this activity, we will take a look at sequencing. Sequences are events that take place in a certain order. Unlike humans, computers cannot think for themselves. They need clear instructions in the correct order.

Coding each instruction in sequence can take up time and space. Coders can use **loops** in their sequence if a certain action happens more than once. A loop repeats the action for a certain number of times or until it is told to stop. See if you can spot the loops in this sequence of instructions for drawing a stegosaurus!

LET'S START SEQUENCING!

1

Draw a half-circle.

2

Attach a long pointed tail to the right side.

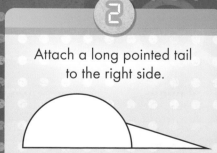

3

Attach a short oval head to the left side.

4

Repeat 4: attach one leg below the body.

DID YOU KNOW?

Some types of coding use "repeat" to call out a loop in the code. For example, if it says, "repeat 4: attach one leg below the body," you should loop drawing one leg on the dinosaur four times by drawing four legs.

5

Repeat 12: attach one triangle to the tail, back, or head.

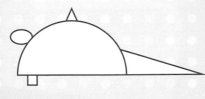

6

Repeat 3: attach one pointed spike to the end of the tail.

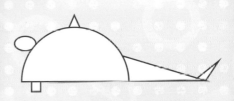

7

Add one eye to the head.

TURN THE PAGE TO SEE HOW YOU DID!

CHECK IT OUT!

How did your stegosaurus turn out? Did it have all of the same body parts as the one below? If your picture turned out differently, why do you think that is? Was there a **bug** in the code? If your picture matches this one, what do you think that means? Was the code correct?

HERE'S A TIP!

Some coding instructions begin with the words "when run." In coding, the word *run* is the command for a computer program to begin.

CODING CHALLENGE!　　　　　_ □ X

Try this next challenge if you want to find out more about the importance of sequence in unplugged coding.

1. Draw a picture of something using different shapes.
2. Create a sequence of steps for drawing your picture. Be specific!
3. Ask a friend or family member to play along. Make sure they cannot see your drawing while they create their own!
4. Tell them your steps one at a time, in sequence, as they draw.
5. When they are finished, compare their picture to your drawing. How did it go? Would you do anything differently next time?

DEBUG THE DINOSAURS _ □ X

Coding requires careful attention, because even a tiny mistake can lead to failure. Programmers who write code must check every little detail. If a program does not run correctly, they must find the bug and fix it. This process is known as **debugging**. Follow these debugging instructions to spot the differences and find the bugs. Good luck!

LET'S FIND THOSE BUGS!

DID YOU KNOW?

Bugs can be as small as a letter that is left out or added to the code by mistake. They can also be as big as lines of code that are out of order. Any type of bug stops a program from working properly, so coders want to keep the bugs out!

1. Look at this pair of pictures. Do you think they are exactly the same? They are not! Can you spot the differences between them?
2. Write down the differences on your piece of paper.

TURN THE PAGE TO SEE HOW YOU DID!

CHECK IT OUT!

The bugs are marked on the pictures below. Did you catch all of them? Was it easy or difficult to spot the differences? Did you compare both a little at a time, or did you study one picture completely and then the other? Programmers look for clues by checking each line of code to discover the bug.

CODING CHALLENGE! _ □ X

Try writing down a set of instructions for a simple but multi-step activity, such as making a sandwich or brushing your teeth. Then, follow your own instructions step by step. Was there an error, or did you write a perfect code? If there was a mistake in your program, try to debug it to find out where it went wrong.

SAVE THE DINOSAURS

_ □ X

This debugging game is for two players. You will start as the coder and a friend can be the dinosaur. Pretend that your friend is the last dinosaur on Earth. You are trying to save the dinosaur from **extinction** by getting it from the start to the goal in the fewest steps possible. Follow these debugging instructions to avoid the bugs and save the dinosaur!

GET SET TO DEBUG!

1

Create a square grid on the flat paved area using yellow or white chalk. Be sure to have six rows of six equal-sized squares.

2

Fill in any 10 squares using red or pink chalk. These are the lava squares.

3

Mark a corner square with an item for the start. Put an X in the opposite corner square. This will be the goal.

4

Have the dinosaur stand at the start. The coder must then give commands to the dinosaur, such as "walk three steps" or "turn right." If the dinosaur hits a lava spot, they must go back to the start!

5

Players can take turns giving instructions as the coder and moving on the grid as the dinosaur. Try different starting points each time.

TURN THE PAGE TO REVIEW HOW YOU DID!

15

CHECK IT OUT!

How did the game go? Did your dinosaur survive, or did the lava win? Were there any bugs in your program? Maybe the dinosaur landed on a lava square when the number of steps was wrong. Or maybe your instruction was to turn right instead of left. If so, did you debug the code by fixing the instruction?

WERE YOU ABLE TO STAY AWAY FROM THE LAVA?

HERE'S A TIP!

Debugging is like using a magnifying glass to look at something very closely. Once programmers have found the bug, they fix the problem and then test the code to make sure the program runs successfully.

CODING CHALLENGE! _ □ X

Make this debugging activity even more interesting by trying it without words! Write the directions down by drawing arrows on separate pieces of paper for each movement. The coder holds up the sheets one at a time in the correct order. The dinosaur must follow the code for each step. No talking is allowed!

TIME TRAVELER ___ ☐ X

Have you ever had to make a decision between two different things? What happened? A computer cannot make its own choices. **Conditionals** are used in code to make sure certain actions happen. For example, IF your shirt is blue, THEN you must jump up and down. Your shirt has to be blue for the conditional to be true. If it is false, or not blue, then you do not jump up and down. Try this activity to find out what happens when conditionals are used.

YOU WILL NEED: ___ ☐ X

- smart thinking!

IT'S UP TO YOU TO CODE YOUR OWN ADVENTURE!

START

You happen to find a time machine in the attic and accidentally send yourself back to a time when dinosaurs ruled Earth! When you land on the rocky ground, the machine makes a loud crackling sound. You think it is broken, but you have no idea how to fix it. What do you do?

IF

you walk away and look for help,

you scream for help as loudly as you can,

THEN

THEN

you come across a dark cave in the woods. In the distance, you hear a roar. Was that a T. rex?

you run, because a hungry T. rex has heard you and is on the hunt for a meal! As you run, you see a cave in the distance through some trees.

IF

you enter the cave to hide,

you hide behind a tree and stay very still,

THEN

THEN

TURN THE PAGE TO SEE HOW THE STORY ENDS!

CHECK IT OUT!

Based on the conditionals you chose, your story will have ended like this:

IF

you chose to enter the cave,

you hid behind a tree,

THEN

THEN

you realize you made the right decision when you find an instruction manual for the time machine lying among a pile of bones. You snatch it and run back to the time machine. You use it to fix the time machine and go home!

you realize your mistake when you hear thundering footsteps. You peek out to see that the T. rex is charging toward you!

HERE'S A TIP!

When you think about conditionals, try to imagine what the result will be if you make a certain choice. For example, when you play a video game, certain actions happen because of the choices you make in the game. Programmers must use conditionals in the code to link actions to other actions when they design games, apps, websites, and more.

I HOPE YOU ENJOYED UNPLUGGED CODING!

GLOSSARY _ □ X

bug—a coding error in a program

code—instructions for a computer

commands—specific instructions to complete a task

communicating—sharing knowledge or information

conditionals—lines of programming language that allow different actions depending on true or false information; conditionals are often written in IF/THEN statements.

debugging—finding and removing mistakes in code

extinction—the process of a group of animals dying out

logic—thinking that is based on facts or reason

loops—groups of code that can be easily repeated

sequences—sets of instructions that happen in a certain order

AT THE LIBRARY

Cleary, Brian P. *Bugs That Make Your Computer Crawl: What Are Computer Bugs?* Minneapolis, Minn.: Millbrook Press, 2019.

McCue, Camille. *Getting Started with Coding: Get Creative with Code!* Indianapolis, Ind.: John Wiley and Sons, 2019.

Prottsman, Kiki. *How to Be a Coder.* New York, N.Y.: DK Publishing, 2019.

ON THE WEB

FACTSURFER

Factsurfer.com gives you a safe, fun way to find more information.

1. Go to www.factsurfer.com.

2. Enter "coding with dinosaurs" into the search box and click 🔍.

3. Select your book cover to see a list of related content.

INDEX _ □ X